BECOMING
MORE

THAN A GOOD BIBLE STUDY GIRL

PARTICIPANT'S GUIDE

Also by Lysa TerKeurst

Unglued (book and Bible study)
Made to Crave Action Plan (Bible study)
Made to Crave (book and Bible study)
Becoming More Than a Good Bible Study Girl (book)
Capture Her Heart (for wives)
Capture His Heart (for husbands)
Leading Women to the Heart of God
Living Life on Purpose
What Happens When Women Say Yes to God
What Happens When Women Walk in Faith
Who Holds the Key to Your Heart?

BECOMING MORE

THAN A GOOD BIBLE STUDY GIRL

PARTICIPANT'S GUIDE

LYSA TERKEURST

New York Times Bestselling Author

 ZONDERVAN®

ZONDERVAN

Becoming More Than a Good Bible Study Girl Participant's Guide
Copyright © 2010 by Lysa TerKeurst

Requests for information should be addressed to:

Zondervan, *Grand Rapids, Michigan 49530*

ISBN 978-0-310-87770-7

Published in association with the literary agency of Fedd & Company, Inc., 9759 Concord Pass, Brentwood, TN 37027.

Interior design: Michelle Espinoza

Printed in the United States of America

13 14 15 16 17 18 19 /RRD/ 22 21 20 19 18 17 16 15 14 13 12 11 10 9 8 7 6 5 4 3 2 1

Contents

About the Study

Have you ever wished you could not only know God's truth but also feel equipped to live it out in your everyday life?

Me too. That's why I wrote this study.

For too many years I was full of Bible knowledge with no idea how to let the truths I knew impact my daily life. I would go to Bible study, leave all inspired, and then come home and have a complete meltdown over spilling bleach on my favorite shirt. Or a kid's bad attitude. Or finding out a friend betrayed me. Or gaining back the five pounds over a weekend that took me two months to lose.

How do we apply truth to this kind of everyday stuff?

We are quick to say all the right Jesus answers in church, around our Christian friends, and in our Bible study. But when the strains of life press against us, do we live as if Jesus really works?

I'm challenged by this. And so I write not as an expert who has achieved a life that authentically reflects Jesus at all times, but as a friend who dares to try to become more than just a good Bible study girl.

Inviting you to accept this challenge is the whole point of this study. I started with a question that many people seem to be asking today. They used to ask, "Is Jesus true?" Books were written about it, sermons were preached about it, seminaries offered courses — all offering up spiritual, emotional, historical, and biblical answers proving that Jesus is true. And I gladly stand up on my kitchen chair with the paint chipping off, shouting "Hallelujah! He is the way, the truth, and the life as He claimed He was."

But now that question has shifted to, "Does Jesus work?" It's great that He's true, but what kind of difference can He make in my life? At first, this question seems bold and self-centered, not even worth answering. I would never want to reduce Jesus to the same qualifications by which I judge a car … that's great that it's the nicest vehicle on the road, but will it get me where I want to go?

Still, "Does Jesus work?" is an honest question deserving an honest answer. The world is literally dying to know.

That's why I decided to tackle six issues that each play a vital role in determining whether or not Jesus works:

- Will Jesus make a difference in my heart?
- Will He help my connection with God be more real?
- What kind of difference could He make in my relationships?
- How do I process my struggles with Jesus?
- What do I do when my thoughts pull me away from Jesus?
- Does Jesus really have a calling for my life?

If we can truthfully answer these questions as I address them one by one in the six sessions of this study, I believe we'll truthfully answer the bigger "Does Jesus work?" question as well.

So, if you're looking for another "keep on keeping on" study, if you're looking for a little more kumbaya in your life, or a good Jesus feeling, or how to play the Christian game better, look elsewhere.

But if you, like me, want to break free from the confines of our Christian arenas and replace the world's emptiness with true fulfillment, please continue.

Lysa TerKeurst

How to Use This Guide

This six-session participant's guide is designed to be used with the *Becoming More Than a Good Bible Study Girl* DVD. You will come together with your small group, women's Bible study group, or Sunday school class; watch the session's video teaching segment (typically about fifteen minutes in length); and then work through the discussion questions provided in the participant's guide. This guide also includes six suggested days of personal study, which I encourage you to do between group sessions.

Part of that personal study is reading my book *Becoming More Than a Good Bible Study Girl*. Though you can have a complete experience with only the participant's guide and DVD, using the book alongside them will be like watching your favorite TV show in high-def color rather than your basic black and white. While the truths are the same throughout, the depth of insight you'll get from reading the book will make your journey richer and even more meaningful.

Finally, you can certainly do this study on your own, apart from a group, and gain life-changing insights. But the rich discussion times that happen in group settings will certainly enhance your spiritual growth.

BECOMING MORE THAN A GOOD BIBLE STUDY GIRL

In My Heart

*The reality is no person, possession, profession, or position
ever fills the cup of a wounded, empty heart—not my heart,
not your heart. It's an emptiness only God can fill.*

DVD TEACHING SEGMENT

As you and your group watch Lysa teach on this topic, use the following outline to take notes on anything that stands out to you.

NOTES

No person, possession, or position can fill up our heart.

When we try to force something besides God to fill us, it quickly turns from a blessing into a burden.

Anything we use as a substitute for God is an idol, a false god.

It wasn't just the people of the Old Testament that struggled with idols.

The same answer their idols gave them is the same answer our idols give us.

With every "if only I had" statement that tries to trip us up, we must replace it with a truth from God's Word.

When I am satisfied with God and filled up with His truth, I can stop having unrealistic expectations from:

People,

Possessions,

And Positions.

DVD SMALL GROUP DISCUSSION

1. As you watched the DVD teaching segment, what is one main point that you would like to apply to your life?

2.   Why is it so tempting to try to get our fulfillment from people, posses-
     sions, and positions?

3.   How does this affect our relationships?

4.   How does this affect our attitude toward possessions?

5.   How does this affect us in the positions we hold?

6.   How can we become more deeply satisfied with God?

7.   With what Bible verses can you replace your "if only I had" statements?

DAY 1

Read chapter 1 of the *Becoming More Than a Good Bible Study Girl* book. If you'd like, record any highlights in the space below.

DAY 2

Complete this lesson:

> I'm not sure when I first felt I wasn't good enough, but my earliest stinging memory of it happened in a place where strobe lights tumbled about in a skating rink full of elementary school kids.... I fidgeted with the laces of my skates hoping to send a very clear message: the only reason I wasn't couple skating was that I had a slight equipment malfunction. But in my heart, a false perception was cutting deeper and deeper into my soul with every beat of the Rick Springfield song. The false perception was rooted in this one flawed thought: You, Lysa, are not acceptable the way you are.
>
> *Becoming More Than a Good Bible Study Girl*, p. 17

1. During my growing up years, I was deeply affected by the feeling that I was unacceptable. Write briefly about a time when you did not feel acceptable.

2. Look up the following verses and summarize them here:
    Proverbs 21:3

    Isaiah 1:13–18

    1 John 1:7

3. How does the world define the word "acceptable"?

4. How does Jesus define the word "acceptable"?

The word "acceptable" can literally be defined as "pleasing or worthy to the receiver." It is who we are offering ourselves to that determines whether or not we are acceptable. If we offer ourselves to other people, we will never be wholly acceptable. People's standards are illusive, airbrushed, unrealistic, temporary, and ever changing.

God's standards are secure, based on what Jesus has done for us and not on anything we try to do ourselves. But we must make the choice to focus on Jesus and His definition of us rather than other people or worldly standards.

5. One verse on this matter that helped me tremendously is Jeremiah 29:11. Write that verse here.

What does this verse reveal about God?

What does this verse reveal about me?

6. Now let's put Jeremiah 29:11 in context by reading verses 12 and 13 as well. What are three amazing promises made to us in these verses?

    •

    •

    •

These weren't just rote prayers being offered up in an obligatory fashion. These were prayers that caused seeking—and not just casual seeking. These prayers caused a wholehearted seeking with a promise of finding God.

IN MY HEART   19

7.   What is your honest assessment of your prayer life now? Circle the description that best fits you:

    a.   practically nonexistent

    b.   canned and obligatory

    c.   friendly but not powerful

    d.   effectively seeking with all my heart

Seeking God with all our heart means to be completely filled and fulfilled by Him. Fulfillment means to be completely satisfied. How might our lives look if we were so filled with God's truths that we could let go of the pain of our past, not get tripped up by the troubles of today, or consumed by the worries of tomorrow?

Let's start today by seeking to be filled up with a truth from God's Word addressing each of these areas.

8.   Use your Bible, the "word search" function on *BibleGateway.com*, or a concordance to find a verse that addresses each of the following:

Shame — (Letting go of the pain from our past)

Psalms 119:31

Hebrew 12:2
Romans 5:8

Temptation — (Not getting tripped up by the troubles of today)

Phillipians 4:6
Matthew 6:41

Worry — (Not getting consumed by the worries of tomorrow)

Phillipians 4:57
Matthew 6:34

Write your three verses on 3 x 5 cards and practice praying them throughout your day. You may even want to insert your name into the verse. Also, ask God to help you see Him, hear Him, know Him, and follow His truth throughout this day.

We'll be building on this activity in session two, so save those index cards and keep them close at hand.

DAY 3

Read chapter 2 of the book *Becoming More Than a Good Bible Study Girl*. If you'd like, record any highlights in the space below.

DAY 4

Complete this lesson:

> How could I have everything I always dreamed would make me feel happy, significant, and loved and still feel so empty? This emptiness made me feel desperate, needy, complicated, full of unrealistic expectations. I quickly became disillusioned. Weren't Christians supposed to instantly have it all together after saying yes to God?
>
> My relationships with my husband and growing family were strained and quickly went from being blessings to burdens. Even though I knew with my head that only God could fill my soul, I still found myself wanting my husband and kids to right my wrongs, fill up my insecurities, and make me feel loved. It just seemed easier to try and get these things from those I could see and touch. But even a great husband and wonderful kids made very poor gods....
>
> The reality is no person, possession, profession, or position ever fills the cup of a wounded, empty heart — not my heart, not your heart. It's an emptiness only God can fill. Anything we use as a substitute for God is an idol, a false god.
>
> *Becoming More Than a Good Bible Study Girl*, pp. 27, 30

1.   Has there ever been a person, profession, or position you hoped would fill
     your emptiness? Write your thoughts here.

     Read 1 Kings 18:20–39.

2.   What was the response of the idols to whom King Ahab and his false
     prophets cried out? What were these idols able to do for them?

     Record verse 29 here.

3.   What was God's response to Elijah's plea? (See verses 36–38.)

     What is your definition of "consumed"? ("Consumed" is the word choice
     in the NASB translation of verse 38, instead of "burned up.")

We have a choice to be consumed with things we think will fill us or consumed with God who is the only One who can satisfy us completely. But, have
you ever gotten caught in the "If only I had" trap?
     If only I had … a better personality.
     If only I had … a skinnier body.
     If only I had … more money.
     If only I had … a husband.

4. Complete the following sentences with anything you've personally strug-
    gled with wanting.
    If only I had . . .

    If only I had . . .

FALSE IDOL #1: PEOPLE

5. Look up Luke 1:78 – 79 and record the verses here.

    Can any person ever do this fully?

    I like that Luke 1:78 – 79 mentions that God can shine on the darkness
    we feel when disappointment and emptiness overshadow us. What will we
    find when we allow God's consuming light to shine on our darkness?

False Idol #2: Possessions

6. Look up Matthew 6:19–21 and record the verses here.

When we set our heart on acquiring more and more things, we'll feel more and more vulnerable with the possibility of loss. What could happen to our heart if we are consumed with wanting things to fill us?

How might our heart be positively impacted by making our desires more eternally focused?

False Idol #3: Position

7. Look up Psalm 119:105 and record it here.

We don't need a better position to get us where we should go. We don't have to figure out our path and jockey to get ahead. What is the only thing we need to direct us, according to Psalm 119:105?

We can replace every "if only I had" statement that tries to trip us up with a truth from God's Word. The more we allow ourselves to be filled up with God's Word, the more consumed—positively absorbed—we'll be with God Himself. The more we are filled up with God, the less we are dependent on other people, possessions, or positions to fill us.

8. Complete this statement: *Because I am satisfied with God, I can stop having unrealistic expectations about . . .*

    Person: _____

    Possession: _____

    Position: _____

DAY 5

Read chapter 3 of the book *Becoming More Than a Good Bible Study Girl.* If you'd like, record any highlights in the space below.

DAY 6

Complete this lesson:

> Satan delights in our feelings of inadequacy. He wants to help us stay there. He wants us to go to Bible study, learn the deep truths of God, leave all encouraged, and then come home and have a complete meltdown over putting nuts in ninety-seven brownies that didn't make the bake sale cut.
>
> He wants us to entertain a very dangerous thought: "Why doesn't Jesus work for me?" When I let my brain run away with this line of thinking, I start wondering why Jesus didn't step in and help me remember the "no nuts" detail before it was too late. I mean, Jesus is quite capable of doing that, right? He is big and mighty, capable of moving mountains. Surely he could have stopped me from adding nuts and ruining those brownies. Maybe He just didn't care enough to stop me.
>
> You see, if Satan can get us asking these kinds of questions, then we can easily justify distancing ourselves from God, once more reducing our relationship with Him to items on a checklist. I prayed. I gave. I served. I did my duty. Now, I hope God does His part and just keeps blessing my life.
>
> But "Why doesn't Jesus work for me?" is never the right question. Instead, when circumstances shift and we feel we fall short, we should ask, "How can I see Jesus even in this?"
>
> *Becoming More Than a Good Bible Study Girl*, p. 41

If you have yet to read chapter 3 of the book *Becoming More Than a Good Bible Study Girl*, the event I'm talking about in the above excerpt has to do with me making 100 individually wrapped brownies for the school bake sale. As I was wrapping brownie number 97, my daughter reminded me of the no-peanut rule for her school. And these brownies had nuts—lots of nuts.

1. Have you had an everyday experience like this where something small in the grand scheme of things made you feel like a complete failure? Describe.

2. Have you ever felt frustrated that God didn't step in and help prevent a mishap in your life, either big or small? Explain.

Looking back on your mishap, how could you have made the choice to see Jesus in the midst of the mess? Did you learn something? Did this reveal a character issue you or your kids might need to work on? Might Jesus be using this to protect you from something worse from happening?

As I look back on my mishap, I can see several things. First, Jesus used this event to teach me how to separate my identity from my failures in life. Just because I fail at things doesn't mean I am a failure.

3. Look up Proverbs 24:16 and record it here.

What is the one word used to describe this man?

The word "righteous" means someone who is morally upright and virtuous. I like to think of a righteous person as being one who makes right choices that honor God daily.

4. This man loved and honored God, yet what do we know about his actions from this verse?

The word "fell" in the Hebrew language is *naphal*. The main idea behind this root is an accidental circumstance or an event. The righteous man didn't mean to fall, but did. Oh how I can relate to this! Interestingly enough, this verb occurs 365 times in the Hebrew Old Testament ... the exact number of days in a typical year.

5. How does this truth speak to you personally?

From this same verse, what do we know about the man's reaction to his mishaps?

How does that inspire you?

A second thing Jesus used the brownie mishap to teach me was to see it as a call to action to pay closer attention to details.

6.   What was your call to action through the mishap you described?

Lastly, Jesus used my mishap to teach me to find the humor in situations. There is humor in almost every mishap if we'll make the choice to see it. The only way I can have the mind-set to do this is to remain secure in God's love for me. I can't remain secure in my perfect performance. Just like the righteous man, I will fall and fail time and time again. However, I can remain in God's love for me. And that's a great place to be.

7.   Record John 15:9 – 11 here. I think this might be another great passage for our 3 x 5 index card collection, don't you?

BECOMING MORE THAN A GOOD BIBLE STUDY GIRL

In My Walk With God

*I keep asking that the God of our Lord Jesus Christ, the glorious
Father, may give you the Spirit of wisdom and revelation,
so that you may know him better. (Ephesians 1:17)*

DVD TEACHING SEGMENT

As you and your group watch Lysa teach on this topic, use the following outline to take notes on anything that stands out to you.

NOTES

We can stop settling for the canned version of both the pineapple and the
Bible.

Ephesians 1:17 gives us an important clue, "I keep asking ..."

In order for Christ's word to dwell in us, it has to get in us. And the only way for Christ's word to get in us is for us to get into the Bible.

What can we learn by studying people in the Bible? Do these stories really lend us perspectives to help us in our everyday life? The story of David is a great example.

David was overlooked by everyone else, but handpicked by God.

It was in the fields of everyday life that David's character was developed to match his calling.

Though David should have been afraid, knowing God was with him helped him fearlessly run straight to the center of God's will.

DVD SMALL GROUP DISCUSSION

1. As you watched the DVD teaching segment, what is one main point you would like to apply to your life?

2. How could it negatively impact your walk with the Lord to settle for canned versions of someone else's revelations? (i.e., never studying the Bible for yourself)

3. What part of David's life spoke to you the most?

4. Put yourself in David's circumstances. What might he have been feeling when his father overlooked him?

5. What might David have been feeling when he faced Goliath?

6. What did David do right in both of these circumstances that can inspire us in various life situations?

DAY 1

Read chapter 4 of the book *Becoming More Than a Good Bible Study Girl*. If you'd like, record any highlights in the space below.

DAY 2

Complete this lesson:

> Ephesians 1:17 says, "I keep asking that the God of our Lord Jesus Christ, the glorious Father, may give you the Spirit of wisdom and revelation, so that you may know him better." We ask and keep asking for wisdom and revelation for one reason alone: to know our Lord better. . . .
>
> I don't ask for this type of wisdom "so that" I can make better business decisions. Or "so that" I can manipulate my circumstances. Or "so that" I can jockey for a better position with more power and prestige. Or "so that" I can feel smart when I throw out the perfect answer at next week's Bible study.
>
> No. It really has nothing to do with me at all. Having the Spirit of wisdom and revelation is purely "so that" I can know God better.

Really know Him. Not just know facts about Him. But know Him in even deeper ways than I ever thought possible.

This is my greatest desire. The one that was planted in me as a little girl when I caught a glimpse that it was possible for me to learn about God, talk with Him, and apply His teachings in a way that makes a difference in the way I live.

Becoming More Than a Good Bible Study Girl, pp. 53, 55

1. What does it mean to know God beyond just knowing facts about Him?

2. What do you desire your relationship with God to be like?

My favorite definition of "wisdom" is this one from *dictionary.reference.com*: "knowledge of what is true or right coupled with just judgment as to action." To truly be a wise person, we have to be filled with truth and be able to discern how to act on that truth.

3. Record a time when you learned a truth that interrupted your thinking and redirected an action you took shortly thereafter.

Let's put this principle into practice today. Here is a truth with great potential to interrupt and redirect us:

> *Reckless words pierce like a sword, but the tongue of the wise brings healing.*

Proverbs 12:18

Using words that are intentional and helpful will set us on the path to bringing healing and wisdom to those we interact with.

4. Notice ways you are tempted to use reckless words and record here how this verse — this truth — interrupts you.

If you read chapter 4 of the book *Becoming More than a Good Bible Study Girl*, I talked about how every word within the Bible has been intentionally and divinely placed, providing us with much discovery and revelation. Therefore I like to unpack Scriptures by breaking verses into word segments and unearthing deeper messages contained within.

Let's do this with Ephesians 1:17:

I keep asking that the God of our Lord Jesus Christ, the glorious Father, may give you the Spirit of wisdom and revelation, so that you may know him better.

5. Record how each word segment speaks to you in relation to the verse as a whole.

"I keep asking"

"the God of our Lord Jesus Christ, the glorious Father"

"may give you the Spirit of wisdom and revelation"

"so that you may know Him better."

Some of my thoughts on these Scriptures are as follows:

"I keep asking"—Praying for wisdom and revelation should be a constant and consistent prayer request in our life.

6. Record here any additional thoughts you have about this:

"the God of our Lord Jesus Christ, the glorious Father"—The word "father" indicates a tender, personal, loving God. He is tender, personal, and loving with me, therefore I can talk to Him—really open my heart up—and He won't get offended or put off. I also wanted to understand why the word "Glorious" was in this passage so I looked it up in the dictionary. "Glorious" means "completely enjoyable." What a beautiful way to think of God.

7. Record here any additional thoughts you have about this:

"may give you the Spirit of wisdom and revelation"—Just asking for wisdom and revelation may help me make a good choice or two, but *the Spirit* of wisdom and revelation indicates the possibility for my every word and every thought to be reined in by God.

8. Record here any additional thoughts you have about this:

"so that you may know him better."—Oh, this is such the desire of my heart: to know God better. The more I ask for the Spirit of wisdom and revelation, the more my actions will be redirected. The more my actions are redirected, the more I will become like God. The more I become like God, the more deeply I will come to understand and know Him personally.

9.   Record any addition thoughts about this you have here:

Now keep going, sisters. Why not make this a regular part of studying God's Word.

DAY 3

Read chapter 5 of the book *Becoming More Than a Good Bible Study Girl.* If you'd like, record any highlights in the space below.

DAY 4

Complete this lesson:

John 20:19 says, "Jesus came and stood among them and said, 'Peace be with you!' "...

The world's offering of joy, hope, and love is fleeting, temporary, and dangerously unstable ... but it can put on a good show in the short term.... So, really, what the world offers—for a moment or two—is false joy, false hope, and false love....

But it cannot offer false peace. It can offer peaceful settings and rituals to conjure up peaceful thoughts ... but not true soul contentedness. The peace that flows despite circumstances can only be found through Jesus being with us. That's why Jesus phrased it the way He did, "Peace be with you!" In other words, "You can walk through anything, My sweet follower, if you realize that I am peace and I am with you."

Why is it so important to spend time with Jesus every day? Because He will give us the exact instruction and comfort we need to handle all He sees coming our way—how to act and, even more challenging, how to react in every situation. It is the perfect measure of His peace, packaged up just for us. With great expectation, we can stick it in our pocket and carry it with us. Instead of being slaves to our emotions and reacting based on our feelings, we can remain victoriously peaceful no matter what.

Becoming More Than a Good Bible Study Girl, pp. 62, 63

1. What kind of peace does Jesus offer? Contrast this with peace the world offers.

2. Why is it important to have true peace?

3. Read Colossians 3:15 – 16 and fill in some of the key words on the following page:

Let the _____ *of Christ rule in your hearts, since as members of one body you were called to* _____. *And be* _____. *Let the* _____ *of Christ* _____ *in you richly as you teach and admonish one another with all wisdom, and as you sing psalms, hymns and spiritual songs with gratitude in your hearts to God.*

What does it mean to have peace rule in your heart?

What does it mean to be "called" to peace?

4. It's always important to look at the surrounding commands in verses. What are some of the surrounding commands with these verses?

Why is thanksgiving tied to peace?

What does it mean to let the word of Christ "dwell" in you richly?

In the book *Becoming More Than a Good Bible Study Girl*, I wrote:

> Oh, how we underestimate the power made available to us when we spend time with God. Our earthly eyes are so limited because they don't allow us to see what is happening in the heavenly realm. A daily battle is being fought for our attention and our devotion. Satan would love nothing more than to keep us separated from the power God gives us during our time with Him. It's time to stop feeling guilty and ill-equipped and start embracing the incredible privilege to meet with Jesus every day.
>
> Remember, devotions don't have to be perfect to be powerful and effective. Jesus just wants a willing soul to come to Him — to verbalize her desire to seek Him and acknowledge her need for Him. (p. 66)

5. What stirs your heart from this quote?

In order for Christ's Word to dwell in us, it has to get in us. And the only way for Christ's Word to get in us is for us to get into the Bible.

DAY 5

Read chapter 6 of the book *Becoming More Than a Good Bible Study Girl*. If you'd like, record any highlights in the space below.

DAY 6

Complete this lesson:

> For years, I looked at biblical truth from afar. I didn't feel equipped to open the Bible and attempt to study it on my own. Instead of reading truth for myself, I only read books *about* the Bible. Or I avoided the Bible altogether and settled for whatever I could glean from other people....
>
> Don't we get into God's Word so it can get into us? So that it can interrupt us, change us, satisfy us? How sad to simply settle for learning facts about the Bible when it was meant for so much more.
>
> *Becoming More Than a Good Bible Study Girl*, pp. 73, 74

1. What does it mean to be pursuing God's truth so passionately that it actually becomes part of our nature?

2. It's not enough to simply read the Bible; we must get into the habit of living out its messages in our everyday lives. How did David exemplify living out the truth of God in his everyday life?

3. Have you ever felt overlooked by other people? How did you react?

Though the Scriptures don't explicitly tell us how David reacted to being overlooked, we can discern his reaction from the surrounding Scriptures, which say he had a "fine appearance" (1 Samuel 16:12). In other words, he didn't have a bitter expression. How does this inspire you?

4. First Samuel 16:7 tells us that man looks at the outward appearance but God looks at the heart. How does this speak to you personally? Do you know another verse about the heart that you would like to record here?

5. Where was David sent after being anointed king, and why was this waiting period necessary?

Do you ever struggle in the waiting times of your life? How does David's story help give you a different perspective about times God requires you to wait?

6. David reveals amazing lessons that he learned during his time of waiting (see 1 Samuel 17:34–37). What did he learn, and how did this equip him for his calling in life?

How can our character be improved by applying the principles we learned through David's life?

7. Can you make any connections between David's struggles and yours?

How did David grow through his experiences, both good and bad?

How might you grow as a result of reading about David's trials and triumphs?

BECOMING MORE THAN A GOOD BIBLE STUDY GIRL
In My Relationships

*Imagine the number of relationship issues that would simply vanish
if we all committed to: (1) use loving words, (2) not judge,
and (3) become secure in our own calling.*

DVD TEACHING SEGMENT

As you and your group watch Lysa teach on this topic, use the following outline to take notes on anything that stands out to you.

NOTES

There is a fundamental need to be liked inside of most girls.

No amount of worldly achievement whisks away insecurities and the fundamental desire to be accepted.

I must operate *with* God's love—I can ask God to show me how I can use my insecurities to my advantage.

I must operate *in* God's love—I can operate outside of jealousy by saying, "I'm not equipped to handle what they have—both good and bad."

I must operate *reflecting* God's love—I must be a woman of carefully chosen words.

It's a great first step to internalize these principles. But what a gift I could give my friends to communicate them and live them out.

DVD SMALL GROUP DISCUSSION

1. As you watched the DVD teaching segment, what is one main point you would like to apply to your life?

2. What feelings of insecurity seem to distract and paralyze you the most?

3. How do these feelings of insecurity affect your friendships?

4. Comment on this quote from the book: "Insecurities should not prompt me to *get* things from others that I should be getting from God. Rather they should prompt me to *give* to others so I can point them to God."

5. When you feel tempted to be envious of another person, how will the following quote from the book help you: "I am not equipped to handle what they have—both good and bad"?

6. What are some practical ways we can become women of carefully chosen words? Discuss with each other what to do when caught in a situation with someone wanting to gossip with you.

DAY 1

Read chapter 7 of the book *Becoming More Than a Good Bible Study Girl*. If you'd like, record any highlights in the space below.

DAY 2

Complete this lesson:

> There is a fundamental need inside most girls to be liked.
>
> We want some people of the female variety to totally get us and walk away thinking we are pretty neat. It's like we carry around a miniature scale. On one side we put our coolness and on the other side our total dorkiness.
>
> Put a group of women in a space to mingle for a while and when you release them from that space, I guarantee many will walk away playing that daisy petal game in their head: "She likes me ... she likes me not."...
>
> Why do I still find myself bouncing around between feelings of dorkiness and coolness in crowds of people? Because, yes, I still struggle sometimes. May I let you in on a secret? No amount of worldly

achievement whisks away insecurities and that fundamental desire to be accepted. I know. I've tried.

Becoming More Than a Good Bible Study Girl, pp. 87–88

1. What does the quote "External achievement never equals internal acceptance" mean to you personally?

   Do you agree with it? Why or why not?

2. What feelings of insecurity seem to distract and paralyze you the most?

If you read chapter 7 of the book *Becoming More Than a Good Bible Study Girl*, you will remember that I mentioned a healthy way to make peace with our insecurities and inadequacies. For me, it is a two-step process: I must operate *in* God's love and *with* God's love.

IN GOD'S LOVE

Using God's Word, I can fill my thoughts with His truths to combat the lies. As I wrote in my book:

> When I feel like that little girl pulling the daisy petals, whispering, "She likes me ... she likes me not," I have to choose to mentally set the flower aside. I'll look up and say, "God, You not only like me, You love me ... and that is enough." You see, I have retrained my brain so God's truths interrupt my negative thought patterns. (p. 90)

Let's focus on a few key verses that can help us to operate *in* God's love. (You might want to memorize at least a couple of them, or jot them on a 3 x 5 card for handy reference.)

Peace I leave with you; my peace I give you. I do not give to you as the world gives. Do not let your hearts be troubled and do not be afraid.

John 14:27

"Because he loves me," says the LORD, "I will rescue him; I will protect him, for he acknowledges my name."

Psalm 91:14

Though the mountains be shaken and the hills be removed, yet my unfailing love for you will not be shaken.

Isaiah 54:10

The LORD himself goes before you and will be with you; he will never leave you nor forsake you. Do not be afraid; do not be discouraged.

Deuteronomy 31:8

Because your love is better than life, my lips will glorify you.

Psalm 63:3

3. How do these verses comfort you?

4. How do these verses help you to press into God's strength and operate *in* His love with more courage and peace?

All of these verses are God's truth. We are chosen people; chosen, as in handpicked by God. God's love is unfailing. He will never forsake us. We have no reason to feel inadequate or afraid when we focus on Him. We must learn to rely on His love to stabilize the places we fall short.

WITH GOD'S LOVE

I can ask God to show me how to use my insecurities to my advantage. Consider this thought from my book:

> Insecurities should not prompt me to *get* things from others that
> I should be getting from God. Rather they should prompt me to *give*
> to others so I can point them to God. (p. 92)

When we take the focus off of ourselves, we have more time to focus on Jesus and others. This thought reminds me of the chorus of a hymn written by Helen H. Lemmel:

Turn your eyes upon Jesus,
Look full in His wonderful face,
And the things of earth will grow strangely dim,
In the light of His glory and grace.

5. How can you use your insecurities to make you more sensitive and discerning toward the insecurities of others?

6. Remembering that when we love others, we are living the truth of God out loud, how can your insecurities, inadequacies, and feelings of dorkiness prompt you to love? What does this look like on a practical, everyday level?

If I was totally secure in myself all the time, I don't think it would increase my qualifications in life. I think it could do exactly the opposite. In essence, feeling like a dork sometimes could be a gift!

A gift that should lead us to operate *in* God's love and *with* God's love.

DAY 3

Read chapter 8 of the book *Becoming More Than a Good Bible Study Girl*. If you'd like, record any highlights in the space below.

DAY 4

Complete this lesson:

> See if you can relate to any of these scenarios:
>
> My house looks great until a friend redecorates. Her clever color combination and crafty restoration abilities have created rooms that look straight from a magazine. Suddenly my home feels outdated and plain.
>
> My kids seem great until I'm around someone else's kids who excel in areas my kids don't. I see her kids quietly reading books that are well advanced for their age and loving every minute of it. My kids would rather have their right arms cut off than read books that are barely grade level, all the while asking me when they can go do something else more exciting. Suddenly I feel like a sub-par mom and berate myself for not making reading more of a priority when they were younger.
>
> My marriage is wonderful until I see a movie starring a Mr. Right character who is the perfect blend of romance, conversation, fashion, and compassion. I compare him to my outdoorsy, T-shirt wearing man who doesn't believe pain exists in the absence of blood ... and I sigh.
>
> *Becoming More Than a Good Bible Study Girl*, pp. 98–99

In each of these scenarios, every blessing of mine seems to pale in comparison. Discontentment is only a thought away.

My heart becomes drawn to a place of both assumption and ungratefulness. I *assume* that everything is great for those who possess what I don't have, and that assumption causes me to become *less thankful* for what I do have.

One way I've learned to divert these ungrateful assumptions on my part is to think this thought.... as often as I need to:

"I am not equipped to handle what they have—both good and bad."

And then I repeat it again to make sure it sinks in ...

"I am not equipped to handle what they have—both good and bad."

1. What does this thought mean to you? How can you relate to it?

When I want the good thing someone has, I must realize that I'm also asking for the bad that comes along with it. It's always a package deal. And usually if I just give a situation enough time to unfold, I thank God I didn't get someone else's package. It was never meant for me in the first place.

2. Give an example where you found this to be true in your life.

When I find myself making comparisons and wanting what someone else has, I must consciously choose to redirect my thinking. Too many of us live with an uncontrolled thought life. It is possible to learn to identify destructive thoughts and make wiser choices. Instead of letting these thoughts rumble freely about in my mind, I make the choice to harness them and direct them toward truth.

3. Think of something you want that someone else has. Have you been lured into thinking, "If only I had *(fill in the blank)* _____ like that person, my life would be great!"?

   Now, practice redirecting those thoughts by saying instead:

   - I am not equipped for her good.
   - I am not equipped for her bad.
   - I am not equipped to carry the weight of her victories.
   - I am not equipped to shoulder her burdens.
   - I am not equipped to be her in any way.
   - I am, however, perfectly equipped to be me.

4. Think about a blessing you have in your life. Do you have both good and challenging wrapped up in this blessing? How are you equipped to carry the weight of this blessing?

   Looking at both sides of your blessing, how does it make you rethink being envious of other's blessings?

   Read Matthew 11:28–30.

5. Look at the three instructions given in verse 29 and define these: Take my yoke upon you

Learn from me

Find rest

Read Psalm 139.

6. Believe that God created you, knows you, watches over you, and loves you — just as you are. Write down the part of Psalm 139 that speaks most personally to you.

Pray this prayer:

Thank You, God, for only entrusting me with what I have and who I am. When I compare myself to others and focus on wanting what they have, it simply wears me out, Lord. I understand that I am not equipped to handle what they have — both good and bad. Thank You for creating me; for knitting me together in my mother's womb. For I know that I am fearfully and wonderfully made, I know that full well. In Jesus' name, Amen.

DAY 5

Read chapter 9 of the book *Becoming More Than a Good Bible Study Girl*. If you'd like, record any highlights in the space below.

DAY 6

Complete this lesson:

"Cross my heart." Those three little words are the container for a big promise. Unfortunately, this same statement can represent a world of hurt if a friend literally crosses your heart and leaves you feeling betrayed.

Words spoken by friends are especially powerful. They can lift us up and spur us on to achieve things that wouldn't have been possible without the encouragement of a friend. But hurtful words can also be the very thing that renders a woman powerless and shuts her down.

The letters and emails I've gotten from women telling me of their devastating experiences with hurtful words spoken by people they thought were friends grieve my heart. And even more so, women hurting other women grieves God's heart.

I'm sure I don't need to share the gory details of how careless words have broken apart friendships. If you're like me, you've probably been hurt deeply more times than you care to recall. And if we are brutally honest, we also can probably think of times when we ourselves have been a lousy friend and caused hurt in another's life.

Becoming More Than a Good Bible Study Girl, p. 107

1. Jesus wants to do a beautiful work in our hearts. Just a brief glance through
    the New Testament reveals why loving others is so high on Jesus' priority
    list for us. Place a bookmark at each of these Scriptures so you can refer
    back to them after you fill in the following blanks:

    *My command is this: _____ each other as I have loved
    you. Greater _____ has no one than this, that he lay
    down his life for his friends.*

    John 15:12–13

    *He answered: " _____ the Lord your God with all
    your heart and with all your soul and with all your strength and with all
    your mind; and, _____ your neighbor as yourself."*

    Luke 10:27

    *And he has given us this command: Whoever _____
    God must also _____ his brother.*

    1 John 4:21

2. Each of the above verses focus on God's love before addressing our love.
    What does this say to us?

    As you read these verses, what friend of yours comes to mind?

    How can you love that person better?

In your sphere of influence, who else can you love better?

It is simply impossible to love another person the way Christ wants us to love while speaking hurtful words to or about them. And loving others isn't a gentle suggestion by Jesus—it's a command. Since our words are such a crucial indication of whether or not we love someone, we would do well to carefully watch what we say.

For others to meet the reality of Jesus in our lives, we must be women of carefully chosen words. There is just no way around this and no justification for not doing it.

Why not commit today to make this kind of love a reality with a close friend. We honor God when we honor each other.

3.   As you seek to become a better friend who loves like Jesus does, search your heart. Realize that what comes out of your mouth is a telltale sign of who you are, whom you serve, and what you truly believe. Fill in these blanks:

- I am a woman who loves _____.
- I am a woman who serves _____.
- I am a woman who believes _____.
- Therefore, I am a woman who watches my words.

Commit to pray for the next seven days:

- I will refuse to gossip.
- I will choose not to judge.
- I will seek to become secure in my unique calling.

Pray these verses during your prayer time:

> *He who guards his mouth and his tongue keeps himself from calamity.*
> Proverbs 21:23

> *When words are many, sin is not absent, but he who holds his tongue is wise.*
> Proverbs 10:19

If anyone considers himself religious and yet does not keep a tight rein on his tongue, he deceives himself and his religion is worthless.

James 1:26

Do not judge, or you too will be judged.... Why do you look at the speck of sawdust in your brother's eye and pay no attention to the plank in your own eye?

Matthew 7:1, 3

4.   Journal what the above verses mean to you.

Imagine the number of relationship issues that would simply vanish if we all committed to: (1) use loving words, (2) not judge, and (3) become secure in our own calling.

And, if you struggle with having friends, as I've discussed in chapter 9 of the book, please spend some time praying that God would bless this area of your life. In the meantime, be the kind of friend you desperately want. God will eventually honor your desire and bless you with true friends. Cross my heart.

BECOMING MORE THAN A GOOD BIBLE STUDY GIRL

In My Struggles

*Three of the most life-changing words
in the entire Bible are "Praise the Lord."*

DVD TEACHING SEGMENT

As you and your group watch Lysa teach on this topic, use the following outline to take notes on anything that stands out to you.

NOTES

Grace doesn't give me a free pass to act how I feel with no regard to His commands. Rather, His grace gives me consolation in the moment with a challenge to learn from the situation and become more mature in the future.

Praise is the key that releases God's character back into even the ugliest of attitudes and darkest of situations.

Where there is praise, God's presence can be felt. Praise Him, not your circumstances.

Praise and thanksgiving work hand in hand to remind us of our position and our promise.

Our position: We are God's people.

Our promise: Thanksgiving moves the heart of God.

I want to live as if both of these — my position and my promise — are my reality. Therefore, I must prepare my mind, protect my heart, and position my perspective.

DVD SMALL GROUP DISCUSSION

1. As you watched the DVD teaching segment, what is one main point you would like to apply to your life?

2. How do you intentionally spend time praising the Lord?

3. Where there is praise, God's presence can be felt. And what does His presence bring with it?

4. Do you praise God in the midst of tough circumstances? Why or why not? If so, how?

5. The story of Peter and John inspires us to make sure our actions and reactions reflect that we have spent time with Jesus. What are some practical ways we can have this be the reality of our life? (Refer to page 138-139 of the *Becoming More Than a Good Bible Study Girl* book.)

6. What was the overflow from Peter's and John's hearts that became the routine of their lives?

DAY 1

Read chapter 10 of the book *Becoming More Than a Good Bible Study Girl*. If you'd like, record any highlights in the space below.

DAY 2

Complete this lesson:

> When my ugly comes out, I am so often tempted to think God leaves me. I wouldn't blame Him. Who wouldn't want to get away from someone with an ungrateful heart and a stinky attitude?
>
> But God is too full of grace to walk away. Grace doesn't give me a free pass to act out how I feel, with no regard to His commands. Rather His grace gives me consolation in the moment, with a challenge to learn from this situation and become more mature in the future.
>
> Grace is the sugar that helps the bitter pills of confession and repentance go down without choking. That's why the writer of Hebrews says, "Let us then approach the throne of grace with confidence, so that we may receive mercy and find grace to help us in our

time of need" (Hebrews 4:16). Grace is the reason I can go to God quickly, immediately—*before* I'm cleaned up—and boldly ask for His help. In the midst of my mess, God is there.

When I am short-tempered and flat-out grumpy, I often don't feel God. But the reality is, He is with me. All I have to do to sense His presence is to acknowledge His presence, ask for His help, and make the choice to praise Him despite my feelings.

Becoming More Than a Good Bible Study Girl, pp. 124–125

Three of the most life-changing words in the entire Bible are, "Praise the Lord." Praise is the key that releases God's character back into even the ugliest of attitudes and darkest of situations.

1. Write down what the word "praise" means to you.

2. How do you spend time intentionally praising the Lord?

    How often do you do this?

3. Try praying Psalm 103:1–5, after filling in the missing words below.

    Praise the LORD, *O my _____; all my _____ being, praise his holy _____. Praise the* LORD, *O my soul, and _____ not all his _____—who forgives all your sins and _____ all your _____, who _____ your life from the _____ and crowns you with _____ and _____, who*

_____ *your desires with good* _____ *so that your* _____ *is* _____ *like the eagle's.*

This passage outlines everything we need during our ugly moments: *praise the Lord and remember how He forgives me, heals me, redeems me, loves me, has compassion on me, satisfies my desires in good ways, and renews my strength.*

4. How do these verses encourage you?

How will you choose to incorporate them into your daily circumstances?

5. Where there is praise, God's presence can be felt. And what does His presence bring with it? Read Galatians 5:22–23 and record your thoughts.

It is important to praise God despite our circumstances.

Praise *Him*, not your circumstances. Watch how statements can gain sincerity when God is the focus rather than circumstances:

- God, circumstances change, but I praise You because You never do.
- God, I praise You for never leaving me.
- God, I praise You for being trustworthy.
- God, I praise You that You are with me in this moment and You stand in my tomorrow as well.
- God, I praise You for being the wisdom I can lean on when I have none of my own.
- God, I praise You for your love and Your compassion that never fails.

6. How can you praise God right now even though you may not feel like it?

Though praise is not often the first or even the tenth thing we naturally think about when the uglies hit, if we keep praise in the forefront of our mind it will become easier and easier to make that choice. Just like any other discipline, practicing it over and over will help it to become more natural.

7. Write a prayer that focuses on Him and not your circumstances.

Though praise is the biggest way I've found to disengage my mind, mouth, and heart from going to ugly places, I also consider five other key factors. Look over the following questions to see which of these conditions might have made you susceptible to an ugly situation recently.

8. Record your thoughts as you read each question:
    Am I overly tired?

Am I overcommitted?

Have I compromised some of my healthy boundaries lately?

Is there sin in my life I'm avoiding?

Do I have things on my calendar to look forward to?

9. What other questions might you ask to determine what triggers the uglies in you?

As I said at the beginning of this chapter of the book, life ain't always pretty. That's a given. And just because you've read this chapter doesn't mean that you'll discover a quick fix and keep your uglies from ever coming out again. But maybe now, at least, you have a glimmer of hope that it is possible to make wiser choices with your thoughts, actions, and reactions.

Praise the Lord!

DAY 3

Read chapter 11 of the book *Becoming More Than a Good Bible Study Girl*. If you'd like, record any highlights in the space below.

DAY 4

Complete this lesson:

> Last summer I had the opportunity to travel with a team from Compassion International to Ecuador. I wanted to see firsthand the work of this missions organization because Proverbs 31 Ministries was considering a partnership with them. To be honest, I didn't want to go at first. But it didn't take me long to realize I needed Ecuador more than it needed me. I'd forgotten how to look at the blessings in my life and really see them as blessings. It's ironic that when we set out to help others, we are often the ones who receive the greatest gift.
>
> The greatest gift I received on this particular trip came when I spent time with a woman who lives in a shanty carved into a mountainside on the outskirts of Quito. Some of the other Proverbs 31 gals and I had to climb a handmade ladder that swayed and creaked as we ascended into the dark cavern she calls home....
>
> When I asked her how I could specifically pray for her, she teared up....
>
> Through the interpreter she said, "Pray for my husband to come to know Jesus and for him to have work. And pray for me to continue to have the strength I need to serve my family."
>
> I was amazed by this dear woman's request. I would have been tempted to pray for God to change my circumstances. Instead she prayed simply for God's provision in the midst of her circumstances. I was so challenged by her prayers and her life. Her kind disposition and peaceful presence was a far cry from my own attitude, which can become skewed when inconvenienced by life.
>
> *Becoming More Than a Good Bible Study Girl,* pp. 131–132

I went to Ecuador to give to the people there. But in reality they were the real givers.

1. Does reading this change your outlook on your circumstances? How?

What are you thankful for right now in your life?

How can focusing on the things we are thankful for change our perspective of our circumstance? Or can it?

Praise and thanksgiving work hand-in-hand to remind us of our *position* and our *promise*.

OUR POSITION

We are God's people. On a personal level I should often call to mind what a privilege this is. Instead of letting my thoughts get swept up in the troubles and inconveniences of the here and now, I can choose to focus on how temporary those troubles and inconveniences are in light of eternity.

2. Reflect on 2 Corinthians 4:17 – 18 as if you were reading it for the first time.

What does this passage mean to you?

The word "eternal" is referenced twice in these verses. The Greek word for "eternal" is *aionios*, which means "having neither beginning nor end, forever, not only during the terms of one's natural life, but through endless ages of eternal life and blessedness." It has to do with the life which is God's and hence not affected by the limitations of time.

3. How does this definition change your perspective of this passage? Your circumstances?

How does it help you shift your focus?

Each time I get frustrated I want to say, "Yes, this circumstance is a bummer. But since I am a child of God, my position allows me to see past the circumstance and find reasons to praise God and thank Him anyway."

In addition to reminding us of our position, praise and thanksgiving remind us of our promise.

OUR PROMISE

God is faithful, and I want to live like I really believe it.

4. How can you do this?

I try not to pray and then walk away. I try to submit myself before the Lord, which often leads me to a mind-set of thankfulness. And then I find that it's often an invitation to personally participate in the faithfulness of God.

5. How can you do this as well? Or how have you done this before?

6. Look up Colossians 2:7, filling in the blanks as you read it.

   _____ *and built up in him, strengthened in the*
   _____ *as you were* _____, *and* _____
   with _____.

   What does this verse mean to you?

   From whom should we be drawing our strength?

   How would this look in your life?

A person whose life is characterized by constant praise and thanksgiving despite their circumstances will shift from just verbalizing their praise and thanksgiving to living it out loud through their courageous stance for Christ.

7. What is the overflow in your life? Is it a frustrated attitude or grumbling? Or is it praise and thanksgiving?

During the course of your ordinary days, do people ever see your reactions to situations and take note that you have been with Jesus?

Read Acts 4:20.

8.   How does this verse relate to you?

Peter and John were so confident in both their *position* as children of God and in the *promise* of His faithfulness that praise and thanksgiving became their way of life. Their post-resurrection circumstances were never easy, often dangerous. They were inconvenienced and threatened in ways I can't even fathom.

And yet their response was to boldly proclaim from their praise-filled, thankful hearts.

> *We cannot help speaking about what we have seen and heard.*
>
> Acts 4:20

It was the overflow of their hearts, and it became the routine of their lives.

How I long to be like the apostles who were so consumed with thanksgiving that people took note they'd been with Jesus!

Let's make sure we intentionally verbalize our thanksgiving to God every day.

Remember, thankfulness breeds thankfulness. The more we practice it, the more we'll live thanksgiving out loud. And the more we live it out loud, the more thanksgiving will become the natural groove of our heart.

DAY 5

Read chapter 12 of the book *Becoming More Than a Good Bible Study Girl*. If you'd like, record any highlights in the space below.

DAY 6

Complete this lesson:

> I don't know another way to say this, so I'll just shoot straight. Sometimes God hurts my feelings. Now, hear me out. I don't mean this in an irreverent way. I very much know my place and I very much have a holy reverence for God....
>
> Sometimes when hurts and disappoints come, they cause a temporary panic that rises and falls in a mini-tidal wave. The hurt feelings can escalate, crest with some hand-wringing and mind-racing, and then slowly ebb away. In the end, you can see how God grew you through it, and you wind up being thankful for that growth.
>
> But other times the hurt comes in the form of a loss that cuts into your heart so viciously it forever redefines who you are and how you think. It's what I call deep grief. The kind that strains against everything you've ever believed. So much so you wonder how the promises that seemed so real on those thin Bible pages yesterday could ever possibly stand up under the weight of your enormous sadness today.
>
> *Becoming More Than a Good Bible Study Girl*, pp. 141, 144

Trying to come to grips with the fact God could have prevented my deep grief but didn't is a bit like trying to catch the wind and turn it into something visible. It's an answer we could chase our whole lives and never get. And sometimes this chase just simply wears people out. They turn and walk away, whispering, "I tried, God, but You just didn't work for me. You hurt my feelings and I don't want anything to do with You anymore."

1.   Describe a time when you have been in this type of situation.

It's understandable, really. We are told from an early age that God can do anything, and we've read the stories about Jesus helping people. But how do we process such beliefs in the face of loss? Whether the loss of an opportunity, the loss of a relationship, the loss of one's health, or the loss of a loved one, loss of any kind hurts.

We too often ask the wrong questions:

Why did this happen?
Why didn't You stop this, God?
Why were my prayers not answered?
Why?

Asking why is perfectly normal. Asking why isn't unspiritual. However, if asking this question pushes us *farther* from God rather than drawing us *closer* to Him, it is the wrong question.

2.   What is the right question to ask when confronted with loss?

In most situations, nothing positive can come from whatever answer there might be to a *why* question. If God gave us His reason why, we would judge Him. And His reasons, from our limited perspective, would always fall short. That's because our flat human perceptions simply can't process God's multi-dimensional, eternal reasons.

3.   Read and reflect on Isaiah 55:8–9, filling in the blanks below as you do.

> *For my _____ are not your _____, neither are your _____ my _____. As the _____ are higher than the _____, so are my _____ higher than your _____ and my _____ higher than your _____.*

The Hebrew word for "ways" is *derek*, which means "journey, path, course, manner, way of life." More often it refers to the actions and behavior of men, whether wicked or righteous.

4.   How does this definition change your perspective of these verses?

Do these verses comfort you? Why or why not?

We can't see the full scope of the situation like God can; therefore, we must acknowledge that His thoughts are more complete and that He is more capable of accurately discerning what is best in every circumstance.

If asking the *why* question doesn't offer hope, what will? The *what* question. In other words: Now that this has happened, *what* am I supposed to do with it?

5.   How can you relate this thought to an area in your life right now?

The *why* questions can be replaced with truths from God's Word.

In time, you can lift up your despair, your doubts and questions, and your feelings of being hurt by God. And with open hands held high, you let the wind blow them all away. But remember: It takes time and it takes prayer.

6.   What have you learned from this chapter that will help you process loss or hurt that is yet to come?

BECOMING MORE THAN A GOOD BIBLE STUDY GIRL

In My Thoughts

God wants us to stand on the absolute truth that
He is with us no matter how our feelings may betray us.

DVD TEACHING SEGMENT

As you and your group watch Lysa teach on this topic, use the following outline to take notes on anything that stands out to you.

NOTES

The problem is that we have been trained to process life based on the way we feel.

But God never meant for us to feel our way to Him.

God wants us to stand on the absolute truth that He is with us no matter how our feelings may betray that reality.

I've never regretted running. The same can be said for my time with the Lord. I have never walked away from spending time with the Lord feeling less close than when we started. I don't stop spending time with the Lord until I've learned or received something from Him.

The less entangled we are in our own self-distracting thoughts, the more effective we'll be for Christ.

Healing is a journey — a day-by-day choice.

When we see Jesus we will be changed in the best kind of way. Jesus will no longer be an emotional figment of our thoughts; He will be so real we won't be able to be anything but completely devoted to Him.

DVD SMALL GROUP DISCUSSION

1. As you watched the DVD teaching segment, what is one main point you would like to apply to your life?

2. How do you process life, through your feelings or through God's truth?

3. What distractions pull you or block you from the Lord?

4. Is it Christian to say you like yourself?

5. What do you obsess over about yourself, and how does this negatively affect you?

6. Have you ever let yourself dare to believe that Jesus would love to show Himself to you? Not in a physical sense but in a spiritual sense.

7. Tell of a situation where you have seen evidence of Jesus in your life and how that impacted you.

DAY 1

Read chapter 13 of the book *Becoming More Than a Good Bible Study Girl*. If you'd like, record any highlights in the space below.

DAY 2

Complete this lesson:

> I used to have the kind of relationship with God where I viewed Him as the One who makes sweeping glances over thousands of people per minute just to make sure no one is getting out of line. The possibility of having God pause in the midst of everyday life to spend time with just me wasn't at all in my scope of possibilities.
>
> Doesn't it seem presumptuous to think God would want to notice us as individuals, to choose us, call on us by name, and converse with us one-on-one?
>
> The answer to this question is yes in human terms, but no in biblical terms....
>
> When I first heard the word "chosen" in relation to God's feelings toward me, I couldn't process it. In human terms, it seemed quite

presumptuous to think God would pause to pay attention to me. My earthly daddy never did. It seemed quite upside down to think that a girl the world ignored and passed over would actually be handpicked, on purpose, by God.

Becoming More Than a Good Bible Study Girl, pp. 152, 154

Yet the Bible is full of reassurances that this is exactly the way God wants us to process life ... as *chosen*.

Read Colossians 3:12.

1. Which part of this verse is easy to skip over?

Read Psalm 25:12.

2. Fill in the blank: "Who, then, is the man that fears the LORD? He will instruct him in the way _____ for him."
    Which part of this verse is easy to miss?

Read John 15:19.

3. What stands out to you most in this verse?

Noticed. Chosen. Picked for a specific reason—a specific purpose. Treasured. Loved. Isn't that the heart cry of every human? It's a heart cry that only Jesus can completely satisfy.

God wants us to stand on the absolute truth that He is with us no matter how our feelings may betray that reality. When I process life through my feelings, I am left deceived and disillusioned. When I process life through God's truth, I am divinely comforted by His love and made confident in His calling on my life.

4. How do you process life? Through your feelings or through God's truth? Explain.

Some days my time spent with the Lord is as natural as having a face-to-face conversation with a friend. I just open my Bible and the revelations are rich, the dialog flows, and the encouragement I receive sends my soul soaring.

Other days, it's more of an effort. When I feel things are awkward or blocked between me and the Lord, I ask Him why and then sit quietly waiting for some revelation to brush across the corners of my mind. Sometimes it's:

- Unconfessed sin
- A bad attitude
- My to-do list tempting me to cut my quiet time short

5. List the distractions that often pull you or block you from the Lord.

Whatever is holding us back, there is beauty in pausing for the One we should seek over all else.

Read and pray Psalm 27:4.

6.   Fill in the blanks as a way of better ingraining this verse in your mind and heart.

"One thing I _____ of the LORD, this is what I _____:
that I may _____ in the _____ of the LORD all the
_____ of my _____, to _____ upon the beauty of
the LORD and to _____ _____ in his _____.

How can reading and memorizing this verse change your perspective?

How should we pursue God?

Read Psalm 9:10.

7.   Put the truth of this verse in your own words.

Remember and believe that every moment spent with the Lord is time well spent. Consider this:

- We go to Him.
- We give our greatest, undivided attempts to get to know Him.
- We ask for His revelation and His help.
- We keep making the choice to do it over and over again.
- And when we do this, God promises He will not leave us empty-handed or empty-hearted.

I used to say I didn't feel close to God, and therefore God must not be close to me. Now, I say: *God is close and if I choose to be close back, He'll rearrange my feelings.*

DAY 3

Read chapter 14 of the book *Becoming More Than a Good Bible Study Girl*. If you'd like, record any highlights in the space below.

DAY 4

Complete this lesson:

> If you want to ignite a heated debate among Christians, ask this question: "Is it Christian to say you like yourself?"
>
> Some say that the admonition to "love your neighbor as yourself" (Matthew 22:39) requires us to love ourselves so we can love others. Others quickly counteract with Matthew 16:24–26 which says, "Then Jesus said to his disciples, 'If anyone would come after me, he must deny himself and take up his cross and follow me. For whoever wants to save his life will lose it, but whoever loses his life for me will find it. What good will it be for a man if he gains the whole world, yet forfeits his soul? Or what can a man give in exchange for his soul?'"
>
> Instead of trying to balance the truths in these Scriptures, I'd like to get to the message behind both of them. The real point isn't to focus on ourselves at all. Instead, our time is better spent learning how to make peace with who we are so that feelings of insecurity don't become a distraction to living our faith out loud.
>
> And believe me, I've been one of those women so distracted by myself that I was rendered ineffective for the cause of Christ. Becoming more than a good Bible study girl requires a heart free of the entanglements of self-distracting thoughts.
>
> *Becoming More Than a Good Bible Study Girl*, pp. 165–166

Read Hebrews 12:1.

1.   What does "hindered" mean?

What does "entangled" mean?

When have you felt hindered or entangled?

When we are distracted by our own thoughts of not liking ourselves, we are hindered and entangled in the truest sense.

But I love that the writer of Hebrews doesn't just present the problem without offering a solution.

Now read Hebrews 12:2.

2.   What are we instructed to do?

How will you do this? When will you do this?

Satan would love for us to pick ourselves apart, to obsess on the negative. When we do, we become hyper self-focused and take our eyes off of Jesus and the mission set before us.

Many of us spend years trying to hide or fix what we perceive as personal flaws. Jesus would love for us to see ourselves as a package deal of unique qualities that He—the author and perfecter of our faith—saw as necessary for the life He's calling us to live.

3.   What do you obsess over about yourself? How does it render you helpless?

4.   As we seek healing and forgiveness where should our focus be?

5.   Read, write, and reflect on Colossians 3:2.

6.   Read and reflect on Psalm 19:14.

Not only will you see God bring good from your past mistakes and negative thoughts, but you will see another layer of your life purpose unfolding.

The more we see our life's purpose unfold...
      ...the more we'll be secure in the person God has created us to be.

The more we become secure in the person God has created us to be...

... the more we'll be able to make peace with liking who we are.

The more we make peace with liking who we are...

... the more we will be able to untangle self-distracting thoughts.

The less entangled we are...

... the more effective we'll be for Christ.

DAY 5

Read chapter 15 of the book *Becoming More Than a Good Bible Study Girl*. If you'd like, record any highlights in the space below.

DAY 6

Complete this lesson:

> If I could give only one gift to every woman on this planet, it would be the gift of being able to glimpse God throughout their days—the miraculous mixed with the mundane. This would radically change the way we think, the way we process life, and certainly the degree to which we trust God. It would make us more than good Bible study girls.

So, I invite each of us into the possibility of seeing God. Not His actual physical form, but rather evidence of His activity. I want us to be women who lift our eyes up to God every day and say, "Yes, God, there are some who seek You today! I understand it is possible to experience You; therefore, I want that more than anything else. I will seek to see You, hear You, know You, and follow hard after You in every part of my day."

Becoming More Than a Good Bible Study Girl, pp. 173–174

"Seek" literally means "to go in search of, to try to find or discover, to attempt, to ask" (*dictionary.reference.com*). It is a word rich with activity and a questlike attitude. To seek God means to actively look for Him and anticipate His activity in everything.

Before we go much further, let me remind you that this part of the book and our study is about becoming more than a good Bible study girl in our thoughts. In chapters 13 and 14, we've covered how to break free from negative, self-distracting thoughts and how to make the reality that *we are God's chosen* the filter for all our thoughts. Now, in this chapter, it is crucial for us to understand how to activate our thoughts about God. By activate, I mean moving beyond wishful thinking for a deeper walk with God to really putting action to that desire.

Read Psalm 53:2.

1. What is disconcerting as you read this verse?

To be honest, reading this psalm breaks my heart. I wish the verse said, "God looks down from heaven on the sons of men to see the *many* who understand, the *many* who seek God." But the word is "any," not "many."

Which gives me a clue that those who understand and seek God are a rare few.

2. With that thought in mind, now read John 14:21, filling in the blanks below as you do.

_____ *has my commands and _____ them, he is the one who _____ me. He who _____ me will be _____ by my _____, and I too will _____ him and _____ myself to him.*

What does this verse mean to you?

Now, I have to quickly insert something here. Just a few years ago this verse would have struck a chord so raw in me, I might have thrown this book across the room. I would have thought, *How dare this religious, rule-following, nutcase of an author write a paragraph that seems so exclusive! God loves all people. Jesus loves all people.*

Yes, this is true. God and Jesus love all people. But sadly, not all people love God. Not all people love Jesus.

These verses are not giving us the prerequisites for having God love us. Rather Jesus is clearly explaining to us that if we love God, if we love Jesus, we will want to obey His commands. We won't be able to help but want to obey His commands. Our love for Him will compel us. Doing so will no longer be our duty; it will be our desire. We'll follow Him not to win His love or prove how good we are. But rather to live in His love and delight in how good He is.

Have you ever let yourself dare to believe that Jesus would love to show Himself to you? Not in a physical sense, where we could see Him with our physical eyes. But rather, wouldn't it make your soul come alive like never before to see evidence of His presence constantly and consistently all around you? Interestingly, the more this happens, the more we desire to be obedient and love God the way He desires us to love Him. It is a beautiful cycle!

When we see Jesus, we will be changed. Changed in the best kind of way. Jesus will no longer be an emotional figment of our thoughts; He will be so real we won't be able to be anything but completely devoted to Him.

3. Explain a specific situation where you have seen evidence of Jesus in your life.

4. Read 1 Corinthians 2:9–10. As you fill in the blanks below, notice the glorious sense of possibility Paul relates to us.

> *However, as it is written: "No* _____ *has* _____*,*
> *no* _____ *has* _____*, no* _____ *has*
> _____ *what God has* _____ *for*
> *those who* _____ *him"—but God has revealed it to us by his*
> _____*. The Spirit* _____ *all things, even the*
> _____ *things of* _____*.*

Did you catch that? "God has revealed it to us by his Spirit. The Spirit searches all things, even the deep things of God."

If we have accepted Christ as our Savior, we have God's Spirit in us. Therefore, it is possible for God's Spirit to reveal to us the deep things of God.

I have heard people who quote this verse focus on the impossibility of seeing, hearing, and conceiving what God has prepared for those who love Him. But now I see that, through the Holy Spirit, God is revealing deep and wondrous things to us *right now.*

And how does this happen most often? It happens in the midst of everyday life using everyday things. Divine mixed in our mundane. It's the stuff all of Jesus' parables were made of.

I can hardly go through anything in life without seeing God's hand in it. And layer upon layer of these constant experiences with God have built a very secure foundation of faith in my life.

So, what do you do if you aren't currently experiencing God in this way?

5. Read Matthew 5:8 and record your thoughts.

Jesus doesn't say in this verse that we have to be perfect or perfectly ready; He just says that we have to get to a place where our hearts purely desire to see Him — and then we will.

Tell God your desire of seeing Him. Ask Him to reveal anything that may be blocking your view.

6. Write a prayer to God here.

And then start looking. But remember, seeing God isn't for the purpose of being wowed. It is for the purpose of:

- Changing us
- Growing us
- Strengthening us to become more than people of knowledge
- Reminding us of His amazing love for us

It will result in:

- Seeing Him more nearly
- Hearing Him more clearly
- Knowing Him more deeply
- Following Him more boldy

We will become changed people who live out the reality of God. And what a glorious sense of possibility that is!

BECOMING MORE THAN A GOOD BIBLE STUDY GIRL

In My Calling

Forgive me for always praying, "God bless me."
Give me the courage to sometimes pray, "God inconvenience me."

DVD TEACHING SEGMENT

As you and your group watch Lysa teach on this topic, use the following outline to take notes on anything that stands out to you.

NOTES

One thing we can know for sure: our calling is not just about us.

We were designed to experiece God.

One day completely with Jesus is truly better than a thousand elsewhere.

God has never asked me to do great things for Him. All He has ever required of me is to allow His greatness to enter me, change me from within, and be revealed through me.

Forgive me for always praying, "God bless me." Give me the courage to sometimes pray, "God inconvenience me."

I long to live a life pleasing to Jesus, not a plastic Christian life full of religious checklists and pretense. I want to be living proof of His truth.

Just as God promised Jeremiah that He would bring His people back from exile, He will be faithful to draw our heart out of the chaos it's grown accustomed to into the sweet stillness of His presence.

" 'Then you will call upon me and come and pray to me, and I will listen to you. You will seek me and find me when you seek me with all your heart. I will be found by you,' declares the LORD, 'and will bring you back from captivity.' " (Jeremiah 29:12 – 14)

DVD SMALL GROUP DISCUSSION

1. As you watched the DVD teaching segment, what is one main point you would like to apply to your life?

2. Do you feel a tug at your heart to live completely with God, but are still uncertain about pursuing it? Explain.

3. What is the most daily way to discover your purpose in life?

4. Why do we often want to settle for less than what God has for us?

5. Discuss this question: Why do we pray—to get things, or to get more of God?

6. What is the beauty of praying dangerous prayers?

7. How can we be living proof of God's truth?

PERSONAL BIBLE STUDY FOR
The Coming Days

DAY 1

Read chapter 16 of the book *Becoming More Than a Good Bible Study Girl*. If you'd like, record any highlights in the space below.

DAY 2

Complete this lesson:

> Life does have a way of eventually coming around. Sometimes it's in the way we hope, and other times it's in completely surprising ways.... Seeing the good come from hard things takes time. But it can be time well spent if it leads us to realize that it is more important to follow God than to follow what *we* think is the best path for our life.
>
> If I could have written the script for my life, I would have written a much shorter route to getting published. I definitely would have left out all the rejection letters and hand slapping. But I now realize the purpose for all of that. It humbled me and taught me the beauty of trusting God to direct my life (James 4:10).
>
> Not getting those opportunities sooner were not God's way of *keeping me from* my calling; they were His way of *preparing me for*

it. This humbling process wound up being thrilling. I found God in deep ways during those lonely days of writing book proposals that were never published and articles that only my friends enjoyed. But God was faithful, and although my ministry was very small-scale for years, it was still fruitful.

God used that preparation time to teach me how to be passionate about following only His plans. Becoming more than a good Bible study girl means waiting for God's timing, waiting for the good He is working in us. And when we're ready to move forward, becoming a good Bible study girl means remembering to help those coming along just behind us. This ensures that our calling is not just about us.

Becoming More Than a Good Bible Study Girl, pp. 189–190

1. Do you feel a tug at your heart to live completely with God, but are still uncertain about pursuing it? Explain.

Why not ask God to reveal Himself to you in the coming days and confirm exactly what He has for you.

The adventure that follows just might blow you away.

Will it be inconvenient? Maybe.

Will it cost you in ways that stretch you? Sometimes.

Does it force you to live life with a less self-centered outlook? Yes.

Does living to follow Jesus at every turn bring joy that you can't get any other way? Absolutely.

It is the very thing your soul was created to do. It is the most daily way to discover your purpose in life.

Write the following prayer on a 3 x 5 card or in your journal and commit to praying it consistently for the next seven days. Feel free to personalize it according to your unique situation.

Just for today I will live this way ... just for today, I am making the choice to not settle, Lord. Just for today, I will not let the subtle influences

*of pride and thinking I know what is best for me overshadow my desire
for more of You in my life. Today, I will believe with absolute certainty.
Today, I will obey You with complete surrender. Today, I will seek You
with complete abandon. For doing this is fulfilling the purpose for which
I was created ... not to bring myself glory by some great accomplishment,
but to bring You glory by making You my greatest heart's desire. O God,
let me make that choice today. Even if it is just for a day—how I long
for it to be more—but even if it is just for today, may it be completely
so. For one day completely with You is truly, truly better than a thousand
elsewhere. In Jesus' name, Amen.*

2.   Why do we often want to settle for less than what God has for us? Explain.

God has never asked me to do great things for Him. All He has ever
required of me is to allow His greatness to enter me, change me from within,
and be revealed through me. Not to *do for* Him, but rather to simply *be with*
Him.

DAY 3

Read chapter 17 of the book *Becoming More Than a Good Bible Study Girl*. If
you'd like, record any highlights in the space below.

DAY 4

Complete this lesson:

> The most logical question to ask in light of everything else in this chapter might be, "So then, how should we pray?" But instead of asking *how*, we should be asking *why*: Why do we pray? To get things, or to get more of God?
>
> I still present my requests to God, but I try to resist making them the focus of my prayers. Instead, I'm learning to focus on three plain-and-simple things: aligning my heart with God's heart; escaping from my own selfish perspectives of life; and listening, really listening, to God.
>
> Instead of filling up my prayer time with *my* words, I want to spend more time hearing whatever *He* might have to say. Power enters our prayers not by sounding powerful, but by listening for even the slightest whisper from the One who is all-powerful.
>
> *Becoming More Than a Good Bible Study Girl*, pp. 202–203

I came to understand a slight flaw in my prayer life. As I thought about the way I prayed, I realized how often my prayers seemed to center around ways I wanted God to bless me:

- God, bless my kids and keep them safe.
- God, bless me and my family with good health and strong, capable bodies.
- God, bless my ministry and help us to effectively reach people for You.
- God, bless my home that it might always be an oasis for those who live there and those who visit.
- God, bless my husband's business.
- God, bless my kids' efforts at school.
- God, bless this food that You so richly provide.
- God, bless our day today.

Now, none of these are bad prayers, if there even is such a thing as a bad prayer. They are honest prayers, heartfelt prayers, common prayers, the prayers of many women who are rising to the daunting task of caring for their families.

But they are slightly flawed prayers because they set my expectations of God to be what I want without taking into consideration the possibility of God's bigger plan.

I make God into One who stunts my growth with convenience and comfort rather than One who grows me into a woman of character, perseverance, and maturity.

1.   Pause to consider all of this. What does this really mean to you? What does it mean to your prayer life?

2.   Read Luke 11:9 – 10 and record your thoughts.

Yes, we want the promises, but we don't want to get any dirt under our fingernails in the process. We want comfortable circumstances, but we resist any transformational changes that might be necessary. Oh, how we want the gifts promised here, but I wonder if the real treasure is to get to the place where we want the Giver most of all.

3.   In the book when I suggested that we should pray dangerous prayers, how did you feel about that?

What is the beauty of praying dangerous prayers?

How might you begin to look at your prayer life differently based on the content of this chapter?

DAY 5

Read chapter 18 of the book *Becoming More Than a Good Bible Study Girl*. If you'd like, record any highlights in the space below.

DAY 6

Complete this lesson:

> I long to live a life pleasing to Jesus. Not a plastic Christian life full of religious checklists and pretense. No, that would be hypocritical at best and deadening at worst.
>
> I want to live completely with Jesus. Captured by His love. Enthralled with His teachings. Living proof of His truth.
>
> *Becoming More Than a Good Bible Study Girl*, p. 210

For this last chapter, journal what going through this Bible study has meant to you personally. What were some of your richest life lessons? If someone asked you what was the main thing you walked away with from this book, how would you answer them?

_____

_____

_____

_____

_____

_____

_____

_____

_____

_____

_____

_____

_____

_____

About Lysa TerKeurst

Lysa TerKeurst is a wife to Art and mom to five priority blessings named Jackson, Mark, Hope, Ashley, and Brooke. She has been featured on *Focus on the Family*, *Good Morning America*, the *Oprah Winfrey Show*, and in *O Magazine*. Her greatest passion is inspiring women to say yes to God and take part in the awesome adventure He has designed every soul to live. But she always chuckles when people call her the Proverbs 31 woman. While she is the cofounder of Proverbs 31 Ministries, to those who know her best she is simply a car-pooling mom who loves her family, loves Jesus passionately, and struggles like the rest of us with laundry, junk drawers, and cellulite.

WEBSITE: If you enjoyed this book by Lysa, check out her website at: *www.LysaTerKeurst.com*

BLOG: Dialog with Lysa through her daily blog at *www.LysaTerKeurst.com* to see pictures of her family and follow her speaking schedule. She'd love to meet you at an event in your area!

BOOKING LYSA TO SPEAK: If you are interested in booking Lysa for a speaking engagement, contact *www.proverbs31.org*.

About Proverbs 31 Ministries

If you were inspired by *Becoming More Than a Good Bible Study Girl* and yearn to deepen your own personal relationship with Jesus Christ, I encourage you to connect with Proverbs 31 Ministries. Proverbs 31 Ministries exists to be a trusted friend who will take you by the hand and walk by your side, leading you one step closer to the heart of God through:

- *Encouragement for Today*, free online daily devotions
- The *P31 Woman* monthly magazine
- Daily radio program
- Books and resources
- Dynamic speakers with life-changing messages
- Online communities
- Gather and Grow groups

To learn more about Proverbs 31 Ministries or to inquire about having Lysa TerKeurst speak at your event, contact: *www.proverbs31.org*

Proverbs 31 Ministries
616-G Matthews-Mint Hill Road
Matthews, NC 28105
www.proverbs31.org

Becoming More Than a Good Bible Study Girl

Lysa TerKeurst
New York Times *Bestselling Author*

Is Something Missing in Your Life?

Lysa TerKeurst knows what it's like to consider God just another thing on her to-do list. For years she went through the motions of a Christian life: Go to church. Pray. Be nice. She longed for a deeper connection between what she knew in her head and her everyday reality, and she wanted to personally experience God's presence.

Drawing from her own remarkable story of step-by-step faith, Lysa invites you to uncover the spiritually exciting life for which we all yearn. With her trademark wit and spiritual wisdom, Lysa will help you:

- Learn how to make a Bible passage come alive in your own devotion time.
- Replace doubt, regret, and envy with truth, confidence, and praise.
- Stop the unhealthy cycles of striving and truly learn to love who you are and what you've been given.
- Discover how to have inner peace and security in any situation.
- Sense God responding to your prayers.

The adventure God has in store for your life just might blow you away.

Available in stores and online!

Share Your Thoughts

With the Author: Your comments will be forwarded to the author when you send them to *zauthor@zondervan.com*.

With Zondervan: Submit your review of this book by writing to *zreview@zondervan.com*.

Free Online Resources at

www.zondervan.com

Daily Bible Verses and Devotions: Enrich your life with daily Bible verses or devotions that help you start every morning focused on God. Visit www.zondervan.com/newsletters.

Free Email Publications: Sign up for newsletters on Christian living, academic resources, church ministry, fiction, children's resources, and more. Visit www.zondervan.com/newsletters.

Zondervan Bible Search: Find and compare Bible passages in a variety of translations at www.zondervanbiblesearch.com.

Other Benefits: Register to receive online benefits like coupons and special offers, or to participate in research.